Goodbye, Jake

By Bam Schildkraut

Illustrated by Whitney Martin

Goodbye, Jake

By Bam Schildkraut

Illustrated by Whitney Martin

Published by
Operation Outreach-USA Press
Holliston, Massachusetts

ISBN 978-0-9792144-0-0
ISBN 0-9792144-0-8

Printed in the United States of America

Goodbye, Jake is dedicated to:

Cole, my muse and grandson *extraordinaire;* Ira, Nicky, Ezra & Renee Schildkraut; Marilyn Wolkovits of Greyhound Adoption Service (www.greycanine.com); and Jake & all of the dogs who have graced my life with their unrestrained love and joy.

Gracias de todo corazon.

"Yippee," yelled Cole as he jumped out of bed. Spending Saturdays at Grammy and Pop's ranch while his parents were at work was awesome. Grammy always made a surprise for breakfast and Pop needed his help with the horses. What Cole loved most was to play with the dogs – especially Jake.

He and Jake played catch with tennis balls. Cole threw the balls as far as he could and Jake brought them back in a flash. Jake was Cole's best friend and never tired of playing with him. At the thought of Jake, Cole felt sad. Grammy told him last week that Jake was very sick.

When his dad dropped him off at the ranch house, Cole walked slowly through the courtyard gate. Grammy was waiting for him. She took his hand and they tiptoed quietly through the front door, past Jake. The red and black greyhound was asleep on his favorite dog bed, the blue one with the soft fuzzy cover. Cole could hear the other dogs barking in the backyard, but he didn't feel like playing.

Cole whispered to Grammy, “Is Jake going to die?”

“Yes, he is. His body is too weak to get well. The veterinarian will come this evening to make sure Jake dies in peace and without pain.”

"Will Jake ever come back after he dies?"

"No, dear, he won't come back. But we can always think about him and remember how much we love him."

Cole was upset. Why did Jake have to die? Cole wanted to cry. He was confused. He felt angry and afraid at the same time. He did not understand so many things about dying.

In the kitchen, Cole didn't feel like eating the blueberry pancakes Grammy had made for breakfast. He pushed his plate away. "You need some energy if you're going to help me with the horses today," urged Pop as he passed the syrup. Cole ate one pancake and picked the blueberries out of another.

After they helped clear the table, Cole and Pop got dressed for barn work. They pulled on their boots and cowboy hats, and headed out to feed the horses and clean up the corral. When they finished with the chores, it was lunchtime.

After lunch, Cole and Grammy took a long hike. The desert was full of interesting things. They climbed to the top of a hill and saw Grammy's neighbor, Ricardo Martinez. He was a professor at the university. He taught his students about people who lived in New Mexico in ancient times. On one of their hikes, Cole and Grammy had found some pottery shards – bits of broken Indian pots that were very old.

The shards meant that people had lived in the area long ago. Grammy had asked Mr. Martinez to look at the pieces to see if he could tell anything about the people who once settled here.

Cole ran ahead. “Hey, Mr. Martinez! Did you find out anything?” Grammy caught up, and added, “Yes, Ricardo, have you been able to figure out who lived here?”

“Look, Cole,” said Mr. Martinez patting the ground next to him. Cole sat down and Mr. Martinez put a shard from a broken bowl in his hand.

“I found that one right here.” Mr. Martinez pointed to a spot under a cholla cactus.

“It was partly covered with dirt, and I had to dig carefully around it before I could see the whole shard.”

They looked at the beautiful piece from some long ago life. It was red on the outside, with black designs painted on the inside. Mr. Martinez showed Cole how to tell the inside from the out by the curve of the shard. "Just like I can tell the inside from the outside of my cereal bowl," Cole said.

Mr. Martinez smiled, "You are a smart and curious fellow."

"Just like his Dad was when he was Cole's age," added Grammy.

"I'm going to be a scientist when I grow up, just like my Dad."

Cole thought for a second and added, "You're kind of a scientist, too, aren't you, Mr. Martinez?"

He nodded yes. "The pot shards are proof that people lived here. From the thickness of the shards and the color of the paint, I think that it was a family from the San Marcos Pueblo. The Pueblo was a city only a few miles from here. Hundreds of years ago it was a large and busy place. It doesn't exist anymore."

"Why do you think so much about people who aren't even alive?" Cole asked.

"I like to learn about people who lived before me. It makes me smile to think that some little boy just like you may have played right here on this spot, and his mother may have served squash stew in one of these pots. It makes me feel connected to them even if they aren't here anymore."

“Thanks, Ricardo,” said Grammy as she and Cole stood to leave. “We’ll take care not to disturb this place.”

“My pleasure,” he replied. “In fact, I’d like to continue working here to learn more about the family.” He turned to Cole, “ Say hi to your Dad and Mom for me.”

“I will.” Cole waved goodbye as he and Grammy headed out to explore more of the desert. The hike took all afternoon and Cole got back to the house just as his father arrived to pick him up.

His dad came into the kitchen and gave Grammy a hug. “Hi, Mom. Did you and Cole have a good day?”

"We had a very interesting hike. I am sure Cole will tell you about it on the drive home." She turned to her son and said, "Cole and I need a few more minutes before you take him home. There's some cold lemonade in the refrigerator. Help yourself."

Grammy took Cole's hand and led him to the place in the living room where Jake lay on his fuzzy blue bed. They sat down together beside Jake. Grammy stroked the dog's soft ears. Jake opened his eyes and looked at her. He sighed a long, low sigh. Cole knew it meant that Jake liked how Grammy petted him.

"Why don't you pet him, too, Cole," Grammy suggested.

"I'm afraid I'll hurt him or make him feel worse," he worried.

"Sweetheart, I know that you are kind to all of the dogs. You know how to be gentle when you pet them. Jake loves when you pat his head. I think that it will feel good to both of you."

Cole touched Jake on the head. The fur was soft and velvety like Señor Oso, Cole's teddy bear. With the palm of his hand, he stroked Jake slowly in the direction that his fur grew. Jake looked at Cole, and sighed at him, too. Cole felt a little better.

“Your Dad is going to take you home soon. Jake won’t be here when you return next Saturday. Would you like to say goodbye to him?”

Cole lowered his eyes and asked, “How do I do that?”

"Well, you can talk to him while you pet him and tell him how you feel," said Grammy. "He'll understand."

Cole got on his knees and leaned down toward Jake's ear. He whispered, "I love you, Jake. I'm going to miss you so much. I wish you didn't have to die." He gave Jake a kiss on the top of his head.

Cole turned to Grammy with tears rolling down his cheeks. Grammy took him in her arms and gave him a tight hug. Cole noticed that Grammy had tears in her eyes, too.

On Sunday morning, the phone rang early at Cole's house. He was already awake and playing with the train set in his bedroom when his mom came in.

"Cole," she said. "That was Grammy calling. Jake died last night. She wanted you to know how good you made Jake feel yesterday when you told him you loved him."

Cole got back into his bed and pulled the covers over his head. He started to cry, but this time he wanted to be alone.

Mom kissed his head through the sheets, and told him to come out when he felt better. When he did come out, they took a long, quiet walk. Mom stopped several times to hug him. She wrapped both of her arms all the way around his back like a warm, snug blanket, and held him close. It made him feel safe when she did that.

The next Saturday on the drive to his grandparents' ranch, Cole didn't feel much like talking. Dad walked him through the courtyard gate to the front door, and waited while he rang the doorbell. The dogs howled when they heard the car drive up, and howled even louder at the sound of the bell.

Pop opened the door, and the dogs pranced and wiggled with delight to see Cole. Cole knelt down to pet the smallest dog, Bella, a tiny terrier who kissed him right on his nose. “No more kisses! It tickles,” he giggled, not really wanting Bella to stop. From the corner of his eye, Cole could see the fuzzy blue bed in the living room. It was empty.

Jasper, one of Grammy's other greyhounds, ran into the living room and grabbed the bed in his mouth, flipping it into the air with excitement like a giant Frisbee.

"Stop that," yelled Cole. The loud, angry sound of Cole's voice frightened Jasper.

The dog dropped the bed and ran out of the living room. Cole's lip trembled. "He can't have that bed. It's Jake's bed."

Dad picked Cole up and gave him a kiss on his cheek. "I'll see you later, pal." He handed Cole to Pop who carried him piggyback into the kitchen where Grammy was frosting hot cinnamon rolls. Pop told her what happened.

"Whenever I see Jake's bed, I feel sad, too," she told Cole.

The three of them ate the cinnamon rolls without talking. When breakfast was finished, Grammy asked Cole to go for a short walk with her.

"First I have to help Pop with the horses."

"I don't think Pop will mind if we take a walk first. Is that alright with you, Pop?"

Pop shook his head yes. “I’ll see you at the barn in a little while, pardner.”

As Cole put on his hat, he asked Grammy where they were going.

“We’re going to the Memory Garden,” she said, adjusting the strap on her hat.

Cole knew the spot. Memory Garden was the name Grammy called the place where her dogs were buried. It was in a circle of juniper trees just beyond the backyard. He had passed by many times on their walks. The four graves belonged to dogs that had died before Cole was born or when he was too young to remember. But now, Jake would be in the Memory Garden. Cole felt a little afraid of going there, but he was curious, too.

When they got to the circle of junipers, Cole could see one fresh pile of dirt among the four other graves.

He knew that Becky, Chloe, Duke and GingerBear were buried there.

Becky, Chloe and Duke were the dogs his dad had grown up with. GingerBear had died when Cole was just a year old, and he did not remember the dog. But he had heard stories about all of the dogs and seen their pictures in photo albums.

The four older graves were edged with rocks and covered with stones. Over the years wild flowers grew among the rocks.

Jake's grave was next to Chloe's. Cole noticed right away that only a few stones were on top of his grave.

"Why isn't Jake covered with stones like the other dogs?" he asked.

"I was waiting for you to help me with that."

"You don't really need my help. You're just trying to make me feel better."

"I do want you to feel better, and I really do need your help. The Memory Garden is a special place for me to think about all of the wonderful dogs who have been part of our family. I like to remember the funny or clever or loving things they did.

Each stone on their graves represents a memory. Even though the old graves are covered, I still remember something each time I come here, and when I do, I add another stone. I thought you might be able to help me with memories of Jake."

Cole hadn't expected this, and thought for a bit. "This is kind of like what Mr. Martinez said about the pottery shards, isn't it?" Then he picked up a stone.

"Jake used to take my tennis balls and hide them under his fuzzy blue bed." Cole laid the stone on top of the grave. He smiled at Grammy, "Your turn."

"One day while I was busy making lunch, Jake sneaked a loaf of bread off of the kitchen counter and shared it under the table with Chloe! Before I knew it was missing, they ate the whole thing!"

Cole laughed and said, "I think that deserves two stones!"

They placed one on Jake's grave and one on Chloe's.

One week later, Cole could hardly wait for Dad to stop the car at the ranch. As soon as the engine was shut, Cole unbuckled his seatbelt and jumped out. He ran toward the house.

"Grammy! Grammy!" he yelled.

"My goodness, aren't you full of energy this morning," she smiled as she opened the door.

Cole grabbed Grammy's hand. "We have to take a walk."

"Right now, before breakfast?"

"Yes, Grammy, right now. It won't take long."

Cole led her along the path behind the backyard.

“We’re going to the Memory Garden,” he informed her.

In a few minutes they were at the circle of trees. They stopped in front of Jake’s grave.

“Grammy, I have a really good memory of Jake. I found a special stone for it.” Cole pulled a beautiful, white quartz stone from his jeans pocket. He knelt down at the edge of Jake’s grave and Grammy knelt beside him.

"Jake, I remember how you used to sit underneath my chair at the kitchen table when I was little. Every time I dropped some food, you ate it up. Sometimes, before it even hit the floor! And Grammy thought I was a real neat eater," he laughed. With that memory spoken to his old friend, Cole laid the sparkling white stone on Jake's grave.

“That’s a wonderful memory,” Grammy told Cole. “I’m lucky to have had Jake to clean up after you.” They both laughed.

As they walked back to the house, Cole said, “Grammy, will Jake always love me?”

“Yes.”

“And will you?” he asked looking up at her.

“Yes, always.”

“And will Mommy and Dad and Pop?”

“Always and forever,” Grammy promised.

Cole sighed in relief. “What’s for breakfast, Gram?”

“Chocolate chip waffles.”

“My very favorite!”

About Operation Outreach – USA

Operation Outreach – USA is a not-for-profit corporation headquartered in Natick, Massachusetts that provides a national literacy and character education program to elementary and middle schools.

Operation Outreach – USA was founded in 1991 by Judith Golden, its current President and Malcolm Stamper (deceased), the former President and Vice-Chairman of the Boeing Company.

Believing that reading is the gateway to success, Operation Outreach – USA offers programs that help level the learning field for at-risk children by giving them books and the confidence to become motivated readers. Operation Outreach – USA uses specially selected books with messages that positively affect attitudes, behavior and character. Operation Outreach – USA involves the school and the home and provides the tools for teachers and parents to nurture and guide children in their academic and social development.

The newly created Operation Outreach-USA Press designs and publishes all new materials used in the Operation Outreach – USA program.

Operation Outreach – USA has reached nearly one million children in schools in all fifty states due to the support of a broad alliance of corporate, foundation and individual sponsors.

To learn more about Operation Outreach – USA and how to become a contributor, visit www.oousa.org or call the headquarters office at 1-800-243-7929.